Incredibly Easy Entertaining

Publications International, Ltd.
Favorite Brand Name Recipes at www.fbnr.com

Pictured on the front cover: Fried Calamari *(page 122).*
Pictured on the back cover: Southern Pimiento Cheese *(page 36).*

ISBN-13: 978-1-4127-2550-7
ISBN-10: 1-4127-2550-X

Library of Congress Control Number: 2007921110

Manufactured in China.

8 7 6 5 4 3 2 1

Microwave Cooking: Microwave ovens vary in wattage. Use the cooking times as guidelines and check for doneness before adding more time.

Preparation/Cooking Times: Preparation times are based on the approximate amount of time required to assemble the recipe before cooking, baking, chilling or serving. These times include preparation steps such as measuring, chopping and mixing. The fact that some preparations and cooking can be done simultaneously is taken into account. Preparation of optional ingredients and serving suggestions is not included.

Contents

**Pastry Puffs with Goat Cheese
and Spinach (p. 20)**

**Original Buffalo Chicken
Wings (p. 10)**

California Quesadillas
(p. 27)

Beef & Roasted Pepper
Crostini (p. 17)

Classic Starters

Grilled Vegetable Pizzas

2 tablespoons olive oil
1 clove garlic, minced
1 medium red bell pepper, halved and seeded
2 (½-inch-thick) slices eggplant, lightly salted
1 (½-inch-thick) slice red onion
4 small (6-inch) prebaked pizza crusts
4 teaspoons prepared pesto sauce
1¼ cups grated CABOT Sharp Cheddar, divided
      (about 5 ounces)

1. Preheat barbecue grill, allowing coals to turn to gray ash, or set gas grill to medium.

2. In small bowl, combine olive oil and garlic. Place vegetables on grill and cook, brushing with oil-garlic mixture and turning frequently, until lightly browned and tender, about 10 minutes.

3. Remove vegetables from grill, let cool slightly and cut into ½-inch pieces.

4. Place pizza crusts on grill, top side down, and cook until warm, 3 to 5 minutes.

5. Remove crusts from grill and spread each with 1 teaspoon pesto sauce. Top each with ¼ cup cheese and one-fourth of vegetables. Scatter some of remaining ¼ cup cheese on top.

6. Return pizzas to grill and cook until crust is crisp and cheese is melted. Cut pizzas into wedges and serve. *Makes 8 servings*

Roasted Red Potato Bites

Prep Time: 10 minutes • **Cook Time:** 40 minutes

1½ pounds red potatoes (about 15 small)
1 cup shredded cheddar cheese (about 4 ounces)
½ cup HELLMANN'S® or BEST FOODS® Real Mayonnaise
½ cup sliced green onions
2 tablespoons chopped fresh basil leaves (optional)
10 slices bacon, crisp-cooked and crumbled

1. Preheat oven to 400°F. On large baking sheet, arrange potatoes and bake 35 minutes or until tender. Let stand until cool enough to handle.

2. Cut each potato in half, then cut thin slice from bottom of each potato half. With small melon baller or spoon, scoop pulp from potatoes leaving ¼-inch shell. Place pulp in medium bowl; set shells aside.

3. In medium bowl, lightly mash pulp. Stir in remaining ingredients. Spoon or pipe potato filling into potato shells.

4. Arrange filled shells on baking sheet and broil 3 minutes or until golden and heated through. *Makes 30 bites*

Original Buffalo Chicken Wings

Prep Time: 10 minutes • **Cook Time:** 15 minutes

Zesty Blue Cheese Dip (recipe follows)
2½ pounds chicken wings, split and tips discarded
½ cup *Frank's® RedHot®* Original Cayenne Pepper Sauce (or to taste)
⅓ cup butter or margarine, melted
Celery sticks

1. Prepare Zesty Blue Cheese Dip.

2. Deep fry* wings at 400°F 12 minutes or until crisp and no longer pink; drain.

3. Combine **Frank's RedHot** Sauce and butter in large bowl. Add wings to sauce; toss to coat evenly. Serve with Zesty Blue Cheese Dip and celery.
Makes 24 to 30 individual pieces

*Or, prepare wings using one of the cooking methods below. Add wings to sauce; toss well to coat completely.

To Bake: Place wings in a single layer on rack in foil-lined roasting pan. Bake at 425°F 1 hour or until crisp and no longer pink, turning halfway through baking time.

To Broil: Place wings in a single layer on rack in foil-lined roasting pan. Broil 6 inches from heat 15 to 20 minutes or until crisp and no longer pink, turning once.

To Grill: Place wings on an oiled grid. Grill, over medium heat, 30 to 40 minutes or until crisp and no longer pink, turning often.

Zesty Blue Cheese Dip

Prep Time: 5 minutes

½ cup blue cheese salad dressing
¼ cup sour cream
2 teaspoons *Frank's*® RedHot® Original Cayenne Pepper Sauce

Combine all ingredients in medium serving bowl; mix well. Garnish with crumbled blue cheese, if desired. *Makes ¾ cup dip*

Shanghai Red Wings: Cook chicken wings as directed on page 10. Combine ¼ cup soy sauce, 3 tablespoons honey, 3 tablespoons ***Frank's RedHot*** Sauce, 2 tablespoons peanut oil, 1 teaspoon grated peeled fresh ginger and 1 teaspoon minced garlic in small bowl. Mix well. Pour sauce over wings; toss well to coat evenly.

Cajun Wings: Cook chicken wings as directed on page 10. Combine ⅓ cup ***Frank's RedHot*** Sauce, ⅓ cup ketchup, ¼ cup (½ stick) melted butter or margarine and 2 teaspoons Cajun seasoning in small bowl. Mix well. Pour sauce over wings; toss well to coat evenly.

Santa Fe Wings: Cook chicken wings as directed on page 10. Combine ¼ cup (½ stick) melted butter or margarine, ¼ cup ***Frank's RedHot*** Sauce, ¼ cup chili sauce and 1 teaspoon chili powder in small bowl. Mix well. Pour sauce over wings; toss well to coat evenly.

Sweet 'n' Spicy Wings: Cook chicken wings as directed on page 10. Combine ⅓ cup ***Frank's RedHot*** Sauce, ¼ cup (½ stick) butter, 2 tablespoons each thawed frozen orange juice concentrate and honey, and ¼ teaspoon each ground cinnamon and ground allspice in small microwavable bowl. Microwave on HIGH 1 minute or until butter is melted. Stir until smooth. Pour sauce over wings; toss well to coat evenly.

Kentucky Style Wings: Cook chicken wings as directed on page 10. Combine ¼ cup (½ stick) melted butter or margarine, ¼ cup ***Frank's RedHot*** Sauce, 2 tablespoons pancake syrup and 2 tablespoons bourbon in large bowl. Mix well. Pour sauce over wings; toss well to coat evenly.

Saucy Mini Franks

Prep Time: 5 minutes • Cook Time: 5 minutes

½ cup *French's®* Honey Mustard
½ cup chili sauce or ketchup
½ cup grape jelly
1 tablespoon *Frank's® RedHot®* Original Cayenne Pepper Sauce
1 pound mini cocktail franks or 1 pound cooked meatballs

1. Combine mustard, chili sauce, grape jelly and **Frank's RedHot** Sauce in saucepan.

2. Add cocktail franks. Simmer and stir 5 minutes or until jelly is melted and franks are hot.   *Makes about 6 servings*

Cheese Snacks

2 ounces cream cheese, softened
½ cup (2 ounces) shredded Cheddar cheese
1 jar (2 ounces) diced pimientos, drained
2 tablespoons finely chopped pecans
½ teaspoon hot pepper sauce
24 (¼-inch-thick) French bread slices or party bread slices

1. Preheat broiler. Combine cream cheese and Cheddar cheese in small bowl; mix well. Stir in pimientos, pecans and pepper sauce.

2. Place bread slices on broiler pan or nonstick baking sheet. Broil 4 inches from heat 1 to 2 minutes or until lightly toasted on both sides.

3. Spread cheese mixture evenly onto bread slices. Broil 1 to 2 minutes or until cheese mixture is hot and bubbly. Transfer to serving plate.

Makes 24 snacks

Devilish Eggs

Prep Time: 40 minutes • **Chill Time:** 30 minutes

12 hard-cooked eggs, cut in half
6 tablespoons low-fat mayonnaise
2 tablespoons *French's*® Classic Yellow® Mustard
¼ teaspoon salt
⅛ teaspoon ground red pepper

1. Remove yolk from egg whites using teaspoon. Press yolks through sieve with back of spoon or mash with fork in medium bowl. Stir in mayonnaise, mustard, salt and pepper; mix well.

2. Spoon or pipe yolk mixture into egg whites. Arrange on serving platter. Garnish as desired. Cover; chill in refrigerator until ready to serve.

Makes 12 servings

Zesty Variations: Stir in one of the following: 2 tablespoons minced red onion plus 1 tablespoon horseradish, 2 tablespoons pickle relish plus 1 tablespoon minced fresh dill, 2 tablespoons each minced onion and celery plus 1 tablespoon minced fresh dill, ¼ cup (1 ounce) shredded Cheddar cheese plus ½ teaspoon ***French's*® Worcestershire Sauce.

Stuffed Mushroom Caps

2 packages (8 ounces each) fresh mushrooms
1 tablespoon butter
⅔ cup finely chopped cooked chicken
¼ cup grated Parmesan cheese
1 tablespoon chopped fresh basil
2 teaspoons lemon juice
⅛ teaspoon onion powder
⅛ teaspoon salt
   Pinch garlic powder
   Pinch black pepper
1 small package (3 ounces) cream cheese, softened
   Paprika

1. Preheat oven to 350°F. Clean mushrooms; remove stems and finely chop. Arrange mushroom caps, smooth side down, on greased baking sheet.

2. Melt butter in medium skillet over medium-high heat; cook mushroom stems 5 minutes. Add chicken, Parmesan cheese, basil, lemon juice, onion powder, salt, garlic powder and pepper to skillet. Cook and stir 5 minutes. Remove from heat; stir in cream cheese.

3. Spoon mixture into hollow of each mushroom cap. Bake 10 to 15 minutes or until heated through. Sprinkle with paprika.

Makes about 26 stuffed mushrooms

Beef & Roasted Pepper Crostini

Prep and cook time: 30 minutes

¾ pound thinly sliced deli roast beef
3 tablespoons olive oil
2 large cloves garlic, crushed
2 loaves (8 ounces each) French bread (about
 2½-inch diameter), cut into ½-inch-thick slices
1 jar (12 ounces) roasted red peppers, rinsed, drained,
 chopped
2 cups shredded Italian cheese blend

1. Heat oven to 450°F. In 1-cup glass measure, combine oil and garlic; microwave on HIGH 30 seconds. Lightly brush top side of each bread slice with oil mixture; arrange on 2 baking sheets. Bake in 450°F oven 6 to 8 minutes or until light golden brown.

2. Layer equal amounts of beef, red peppers and cheese over toasted bread. Return to oven; bake an additional 2 to 4 minutes or until cheese is melted. Serve immediately. *Makes about 36 appetizers*

Cook's Tip: Bread may be toasted ahead of time; store in airtight container.

Favorite recipe from **National Cattlemen's Beef Association on behalf of The Beef Checkoff**

Sausage Pinwheels

2 cups biscuit mix
½ cup milk
¼ cup butter or margarine, melted
1 pound BOB EVANS® Original Recipe Roll Sausage

Combine biscuit mix, milk and butter in large bowl until blended. Refrigerate 30 minutes. Divide dough into two portions. Roll out one portion on floured surface to ⅛-inch-thick rectangle, about 10×7 inches. Spread with half the sausage. Roll lengthwise into long roll. Repeat with remaining dough and sausage. Place rolls in freezer until firm enough to cut easily. Preheat oven to 400°F. Cut rolls into thin slices. Place on *ungreased* baking sheets. Bake 15 minutes or until golden brown. Serve hot. Refrigerate leftovers. *Makes 48 pinwheels*

Note: This recipe can be doubled. Refreeze after slicing. When ready to serve, thaw slices in refrigerator and bake.

*Tip

Biscuit mix is a combination of flour, salt, baking powder or soda, shortening and occasionally sugar. It is used to make a number of recipes from biscuits and rolls to cookies and pie crusts.

Pastry Puffs with Goat Cheese and Spinach

1 (12-ounce) package BOB EVANS® Original Links
30 to 40 leaves fresh spinach
1 (17¾-ounce) package frozen puff pastry sheets, thawed according to package directions
⅓ cup goat cheese*
3 tablespoons Dijon mustard

For a milder flavor, substitute plain or herb cream cheese for goat cheese.

Cook sausage in large skillet until browned. Drain on paper towels; let cool. Steam spinach; let cool. Preheat oven to 375°F. Cut 1 pastry sheet evenly into 9 squares. Cut 5 additional squares from second sheet (remaining pastry may be refrozen for future use). Stretch or roll squares slightly to form rectangles. Line each rectangle with 2 or 3 spinach leaves, leaving ¼ inch on 1 short end to seal edges. Spread about 1 teaspoon goat cheese over spinach; spread ½ teaspoon mustard over goat cheese. Arrange sausage across short end and roll up pastry and filling, pressing to seal edges. Place on *ungreased* baking sheet, seam sides down. Bake 14 to 16 minutes or until golden. Cut each puff into halves or thirds. Refrigerate leftovers.   *Makes 28 to 42 appetizers*

Note: Pastry puffs may be made ahead and refrigerated overnight or frozen up to 1 month. Reheat in oven when ready to serve.

Celebration Cheese Ball

2 packages (8 ounces each) cream cheese, softened
⅓ cup mayonnaise
¼ cup grated Parmesan cheese
2 tablespoons finely chopped carrot
1 tablespoon finely chopped red onion
1½ teaspoons prepared horseradish
¼ teaspoon salt
½ cup chopped pecans or walnuts
Assorted crackers and breadsticks

1. Combine all ingredients except pecans and crackers in medium bowl. Cover and refrigerate until firm.

2. Shape cheese mixture into a ball; roll in pecans. Wrap cheese ball in plastic wrap and refrigerate at least 1 hour. Serve with assorted crackers and breadsticks. *Makes about 2½ cups spread*

*Tip

There are many choices to serve with a cheese ball besides crackers. Try crunchy vegetables like carrot sticks, celery sticks and cauliflower florets. You may also like the salty-sweet combination of cheese with slices of pears or apples. Before serving, dip the cut fruit into a mixture of 1 cup of water and 1 teaspoon lemon juice to prevent the slices from browning.

Oysters
Romano

12 oysters, shucked and on the half shell
2 slices bacon, cut into 12 (1-inch) pieces
½ cup Italian-seasoned dry bread crumbs
2 tablespoons butter or margarine, melted
½ teaspoon garlic salt
6 tablespoons grated Romano or Parmesan cheese
Fresh chives (optional)

1. Preheat oven to 375°F. Place shells with oysters on baking sheet. Top each oyster with 1 piece bacon. Bake 10 minutes or until bacon is crisp.

2. Meanwhile, combine bread crumbs, butter and garlic salt in small bowl. Spoon mixture over oysters; top with cheese. Bake 5 to 10 minutes or until cheese melts. Garnish with chives. *Makes 12 oysters*

Smoked Salmon Appetizers

¼ cup reduced-fat cream cheese, softened
1 tablespoon chopped fresh dill *or* 1 teaspoon dried dill weed
⅛ teaspoon ground red pepper
4 ounces thinly sliced smoked salmon or lox
24 melba toast rounds or other low-fat crackers
Fresh dill sprigs and chopped red onion (optional)

1. Combine cream cheese, dill and red pepper in small bowl; mix well. Spread evenly over each slice of salmon. Roll up salmon slices jelly-roll style. Place on plate; cover with plastic wrap. Chill at least 1 hour or up to 4 hours before serving.

2. Cut salmon rolls crosswise into ¾-inch pieces with sharp knife. Place pieces, cut side down, on melba rounds. Garnish each salmon roll with dill and onion. Serve cold or at room temperature.

Makes about 2 dozen appetizers

Festive Franks

1 can (8 ounces) crescent roll dough
2 tablespoons barbecue sauce
⅓ cup finely shredded sharp Cheddar cheese
8 hot dogs
¼ teaspoon poppy seeds (optional)
   Additional barbecue sauce (optional)

1. Preheat oven to 350°F. Spray baking sheet with nonstick cooking spray; set aside.

2. Unroll dough and separate into 8 triangles. Cut each triangle in half lengthwise to make 2 triangles. Spread barbecue sauce over each triangle. Sprinkle with cheese.

3. Cut each hot dog in half; trim off rounded ends. Place one hot dog piece at large end of one dough triangle. Roll up jelly-roll style from wide end. Place point-side down on prepared baking sheet. Sprinkle with poppy seeds, if desired. Repeat with remaining hot dog pieces and dough.

4. Bake 13 minutes or until golden brown. Cool 1 to 2 minutes on baking sheet. Serve with additional barbecue sauce for dipping, if desired.

Makes 16 appetizers

California Quesadillas

Prep Time: 20 minutes • **Cook Time:** 5 minutes

- **1 small ripe avocado**
- **2 packages (3 ounces each) cream cheese, softened**
- **3 tablespoons _Frank's® RedHot®_ Original Cayenne Pepper Sauce**
- **¼ cup minced fresh cilantro leaves**
- **16 (6-inch) flour tortillas (2 packages)**
- **1 cup (4 ounces) shredded Cheddar or Monterey Jack cheese**
- **½ cup finely chopped green onions**
- **Sour cream (optional)**

1. Halve avocado and remove pit. Scoop out flesh into food processor or bowl of electric mixer. Add cream cheese and **_Frank's RedHot_** Sauce. Cover and process or beat until smooth. Add cilantro; process or beat until well blended. Spread rounded tablespoon avocado mixture onto each tortilla. Sprinkle half the tortillas with cheese and onions, dividing evenly. Top with remaining tortillas; press gently.

2. Place tortillas on oiled grid. Grill over medium coals 5 minutes or until cheese melts and tortillas are lightly browned, turning once. Cut into triangles. Serve with sour cream, if desired. Garnish as desired.

Makes 8 appetizer servings

Note: You may serve avocado mixture as a dip with tortilla chips.

Mini Sausage Quiches

½ cup butter or margarine, softened
3 ounces cream cheese, softened
1 cup all-purpose flour
½ pound BOB EVANS® Italian Roll Sausage
1 cup (4 ounces) shredded Swiss cheese
1 tablespoon snipped fresh chives
2 eggs
1 cup half-and-half
¼ teaspoon salt
Dash cayenne pepper

Beat butter and cream cheese in medium bowl until creamy. Blend in flour; refrigerate 1 hour. Roll into 24 (1-inch) balls; press each into ungreased mini-muffin cup to form pastry shell. Preheat oven to 375°F. To prepare filling, crumble sausage into small skillet. Cook over medium heat until browned, stirring occasionally. Drain off any drippings. Sprinkle evenly into pastry shells in muffin cups; sprinkle with Swiss cheese and chives. Whisk eggs, half-and-half, salt and cayenne until blended; pour into pastry shells. Bake 20 to 30 minutes or until set. Remove from pans. Serve hot. Refrigerate leftovers. *Makes 24 appetizers*

*Tip

Pour mixture into 12 standard (2½-inch) muffin cups to make larger individual quiches. Serve for breakfast.

Chunky Pinto Bean
Dip (p. 34)

Southern Pimiento
Cheese (p. 36)

Cucumber-Dill
Dip (p. 42)

Spicy Thai Satay
Dip (p. 38)

Dips & Spreads

Creamy Artichoke-Parmesan Dip

2 cans (14 ounces each) artichoke hearts, drained and chopped
2 cups (8 ounces) shredded mozzarella cheese
1½ cups grated Parmesan cheese
1½ cups mayonnaise
½ cup finely chopped onion
½ teaspoon dried oregano
¼ teaspoon garlic powder
4 rounds pita bread
Assorted cut-up vegetables

Slow Cooker Directions

1. Combine artichokes, cheeses, mayonnaise, onion, oregano and garlic powder in slow cooker; mix well.

2. Cover; cook on LOW 2 hours.

3. Meanwhile, cut pita into wedges. Arrange pita and vegetables on platter; serve with warm dip.

Makes 4 cups dip

Ragú Fondue

Prep Time: 10 minutes • **Cook Time:** 10 minutes

1 jar (1 pound 10 ounces) RAGÚ® Organic Pasta Sauce
Assorted Dippers (cubed cheese, blanched vegetables, cooked tortellini, garlic bread cubes, meatballs)

In 2-quart saucepan, heat Pasta Sauce over medium heat. Turn into fondue pot or serving dish and serve warm with Assorted Dippers.

Makes 6 servings

Chunky Pinto Bean Dip

Prep Time: 12 minutes • Cook Time: 5 to 6 hours

2 cans (15 ounces each) pinto beans, rinsed and drained
1 can (14½ ounces) diced tomatoes with mild green chiles
1 cup chopped onion
⅔ cup chunky salsa
1 tablespoon vegetable oil
1½ teaspoons minced garlic
1 teaspoon ground coriander
1 teaspoon ground cumin
1½ cups (6 ounces) shredded Mexican cheese blend or Cheddar cheese
¼ cup chopped cilantro
   Blue corn or other tortilla chips
   Assorted raw vegetables

Slow Cooker Directions

1. Combine beans, tomatoes, onion, salsa, oil, garlic, coriander and cumin in slow cooker.

2. Cover; cook on LOW 5 to 6 hours or until onion is tender.

3. Partially mash bean mixture with potato masher. Stir in cheese and cilantro. Serve at room temperature with chips and vegetables.

Makes about 5 cups dip

Hot French Onion Dip

1 envelope LIPTON® RECIPE SECRETS® Onion Soup Mix
1 container (16 ounces) sour cream
2 cups shredded Swiss cheese (about 8 ounces), divided
¼ cup HELLMANN'S® or BEST FOODS® Real Mayonnaise

1. Preheat oven to 375°F. In 1-quart casserole, combine soup mix, sour cream, 1¾ cups Swiss cheese and mayonnaise.

2. Bake uncovered 20 minutes or until heated through. Sprinkle with remaining ¼ cup cheese.

3. Serve, if desired, with sliced French bread or your favorite dippers.

Makes 2 cups dip

Southern Pimiento Cheese

Prep Time: 15 minutes • **Chill Time:** 30 minutes

1 package (3 ounces) cream cheese, softened
⅓ cup HELLMANN'S® or BEST FOODS® Real Mayonnaise
2 cups shredded cheddar cheese (about 8 ounces)
½ cup drained and chopped pimientos (about 4 ounces)
½ cup finely chopped green onions
¼ cup finely chopped pimiento-stuffed green olives
1 teaspoon LAWRY'S® Garlic Powder with Parsley
1 teaspoon paprika

In medium bowl, with wire whisk, beat cream cheese and Hellmann's or Best Foods Real Mayonnaise until smooth. Stir in remaining ingredients until blended. Chill until ready to serve. Serve at room temperature and, if desired, with crackers or party-size bread. *Makes 2¼ cups spread*

Olive Tapenade Dip

Prep Time: 10 minutes

1½ cups (10-ounce jar) pitted kalamata olives
3 tablespoons olive oil
3 tablespoons *French's*® Spicy Brown Mustard
1 tablespoon minced fresh rosemary leaves *or* 1 teaspoon dried rosemary leaves
1 teaspoon minced garlic

1. Place all ingredients in food processor. Process until puréed.
2. Serve with vegetable crudités or pita chips.

Makes 4 (¼-cup) servings

Tip: To pit olives, place in plastic bag. Gently tap with wooden mallet or rolling pin until olives split open. Remove pits.

Spicy Thai Satay Dip

Prep Time: 10 minutes

⅓ cup peanut butter
⅓ cup *French's*® Honey Dijon Mustard
⅓ cup fat-free chicken broth
1 tablespoon chopped peeled fresh ginger
1 tablespoon honey
1 tablespoon *Frank's*® *RedHot*® Cayenne Pepper Sauce
1 tablespoon teriyaki sauce
1 tablespoon grated orange peel
2 cloves garlic, minced

1. Combine all ingredients in large bowl. Cover and refrigerate.
2. Serve with vegetables, chips or grilled meats.

Makes 4 (¼-cup) servings

Taco
Dip

12 ounces cream cheese, softened
½ cup sour cream
2 teaspoons chili powder
1½ teaspoons ground cumin
⅛ teaspoon ground red pepper
½ cup salsa
Crisp salad greens
1 cup (4 ounces) shredded Cheddar cheese
1 cup (4 ounces) shredded Monterey Jack cheese
½ cup diced plum tomatoes
⅓ cup sliced green onions
¼ cup sliced pitted ripe olives
¼ cup sliced pimiento-stuffed green olives
Tortilla chips or blue corn chips for serving

1. Combine cream cheese, sour cream, chili powder, cumin and pepper in large bowl; mix until well blended. Stir in salsa.

2. Spread dip onto serving platter lined with greens. Top with cheeses, tomatoes, green onions, and olives.

3. Serve with tortilla chips and blue corn chips.   *Makes 10 servings*

*Tip

Ripe olives are commonly referred to as black olives. Green or Spanish olives are unripe and are often stuffed with pimientos or jalapeño peppers. Opened jars of olives should be kept refrigerated in their brine in a tightly covered container. Olives will keep for several weeks. Unopened containers of olives can be stored for up to two years.

Fresh Fruit with Creamy Lime Dipping Sauce

2 tablespoons lime juice
1 small jicama, peeled and cut into ½-inch-thick strips 3 to 4 inches long
2 pounds watermelon, rind removed, and fruit cut into ½-inch-thick wedges 2 to 3 inches wide
½ small pineapple, peeled, halved lengthwise and cut crosswise into wedges
1 ripe papaya, peeled, seeded and sliced crosswise
   Creamy Lime Dipping Sauce (recipe follows)

Combine lime juice and jicama in large bowl; toss. Drain. Arrange jicama, watermelon, pineapple and papaya on large platter. Serve with Creamy Lime Dipping Sauce.
Makes 12 servings

Creamy Lime Dipping Sauce

1 container (6 ounces) vanilla yogurt
2 tablespoons minced fresh cilantro
2 tablespoons lime juice
1 tablespoon minced jalapeño pepper*

*Jalapeño peppers can sting and irritate the skin, so wear rubber gloves when handling peppers and do not touch your eyes.

Combine all ingredients in small bowl; mix well to combine.
Makes about 1 cup

Asian Peanut Butter Dip

3 tablespoons reduced-fat creamy peanut butter
2 tablespoons apple butter
2 tablespoons fat-free (skim) milk
1 tablespoon reduced-sodium soy sauce
1½ teaspoons lime juice
10 stalks celery, cut into fourths

Combine peanut butter, apple butter, milk and soy sauce in small bowl; whisk together until very smooth. Store, tightly sealed, in refrigerator. Serve with celery. *Makes 5 servings*

Travel Tip: Divide dip between 5 individual plastic containers; cover tightly. Divide celery between 5 small resealable plastic bags. Store in cooler with ice.

Cucumber-Dill Dip

Salt
1 cucumber, peeled, seeded and finely chopped
6 green onions, white parts only, chopped
1 package (3 ounces) reduced-fat cream cheese
1 cup plain yogurt
2 tablespoons fresh dill *or* **1 tablespoon dried dill weed**
Fresh dill sprigs (optional)

1. Lightly salt cucumber in small bowl; toss. Refrigerate 1 hour. Drain cucumber; dry on paper towels. Return cucumbers to bowl and add onions. Set aside.

2. Place cream cheese, yogurt and dill in food processor or blender; process until smooth. Stir into cucumber mixture. Transfer to serving bowl. Cover; refrigerate 1 hour. Garnish with fresh dill.

Makes about 2 cups dip

Pizza Fondue

Prep Time: 15 minutes • **Cook Time:** 3 to 4 hours

½ **pound bulk Italian sausage**
1 **cup chopped onion**
2 **jars (26 ounces each) meatless pasta sauce**
4 **ounces thinly sliced ham, finely chopped**
1 **package (3 ounces) sliced pepperoni, finely chopped**
¼ **teaspoon red pepper flakes**
1 **pound mozzarella cheese, cut into ¾-inch cubes**
1 **loaf Italian or French bread, cut into 1-inch cubes**

Slow Cooker Directions

1. Cook sausage and onion in large skillet over medium-high heat until sausage is browned, stirring to break up meat. Drain fat. Transfer sausage mixture to slow cooker.

2. Stir in pasta sauce, ham, pepperoni and pepper flakes. Cover; cook on LOW 3 to 4 hours.

3. Serve fondue with cheese and bread cubes.

Makes 20 to 25 servings

Smokey Chipotle Party Dip

¾ **cup sour cream**
¾ **cup mayonnaise**
¾ **cup ORTEGA® Salsa, any variety**
1 **package (1.25 ounces) ORTEGA Smokey Chipotle Taco Seasoning Mix**
Chopped tomatoes, chopped cilantro, chopped olives and shredded Cheddar cheese
Blue corn tortilla chips

COMBINE all ingredients except chips; stir until blended.

SPREAD dip in shallow serving dish or pie plate and sprinkle with tomatoes, cilantro, olives or cheese, if desired. Serve with tortilla chips.

Makes 2¼ cups dip

Note: This flavorful dip is ready to go as soon as you make it, but can also be refrigerated and made up to two days before serving.

*Tip

Chipotle chile peppers are dried, smoked jalapeño peppers with reddish-brown skins. They are often found bagged in the ethnic aisle of the supermarket. Chipotles can also be found canned in adobo sauce, perfect for adding to chili, soups and stews.

Ortega® Green Chile Guacamole

2 medium very ripe avocados, seeded, peeled and mashed
1 can (4 ounces) ORTEGA® Diced Green Chiles
2 large green onions, chopped
2 tablespoons olive oil
1 teaspoon lime juice
1 clove garlic, finely chopped
¼ teaspoon salt
   Tortilla chips

COMBINE avocados, chiles, green onions, olive oil, lime juice, garlic and salt in medium bowl. Cover; refrigerate for at least 1 hour. Serve with chips.   *Makes 2 cups*

*Tip

This all-time favorite dip can be used in tacos, burritos, tamales, chimichangas or combined with ORTEGA Salsa for a spicy salad dressing.

Cheesy Mustard Dip

Prep Time: 15 minutes

1 container (8 ounces) whipped cream cheese
¼ cup milk
**3 tablespoons *French's*® Spicy Brown Mustard or Honey
   Mustard**
2 tablespoons mayonnaise
2 tablespoons minced green onions

Combine ingredients for dip in medium bowl; mix until well blended.
                               Makes 8 servings (about 1¼ cups dip)

Five-Layered Mexican Dip

½ cup low fat sour cream

½ cup **GUILTLESS GOURMET®** Salsa (Roasted Red Pepper or Southwestern Grill)

1 jar (16 ounces) **GUILTLESS GOURMET®** Black Bean Dip (Spicy or Mild)

2 cups shredded lettuce

½ cup chopped tomato

¼ cup (1 ounce) shredded sharp Cheddar cheese

Chopped fresh cilantro and cilantro sprigs (optional)

1 large bag (7 ounces) **GUILTLESS GOURMET®** Baked Tortilla Chips (yellow, white or blue corn)

Mix together sour cream and salsa in small bowl. Spread bean dip in shallow glass bowl. Top with sour cream-salsa mixture, spreading to cover bean dip.* Just before serving, top with lettuce, tomato and cheese. Garnish with cilantro, if desired. Serve with tortilla chips.

Makes 8 servings

Dip may be prepared to this point; cover and refrigerate up to 24 hours.

Hot Artichoke Dip

Prep Time: 5 minutes • **Bake Time:** 30 minutes

1 envelope LIPTON® RECIPE SECRETS® Onion Soup Mix*
1 can (14 ounces) artichoke hearts, drained and chopped
1 cup HELLMANN'S® or BEST FOODS® Real Mayonnaise
1 container (8 ounces) sour cream
**1 cup shredded Swiss or mozzarella cheese (about
    4 ounces)**

*Also terrific with LIPTON® RECIPE SECRETS® Savory Herb with Garlic, Golden Onion or Onion Mushroom Soup Mix.

1. Preheat oven to 350°F. In 1-quart casserole, combine all ingredients.

2. Bake uncovered, 30 minutes or until heated through.

3. Serve with your favorite dippers.   *Makes 3 cups dip*

Cold Artichoke Dip: Omit Swiss cheese. Stir in, if desired, ¼ cup grated Parmesan cheese. Do not bake.

*Tip

When serving hot dip for a party, try baking it in 2 smaller casseroles. When the first casserole is empty, replace it with the second one, fresh from the oven.

Shrimp Pâté
(p. 68)

Quick Pickled Green
Beans (p. 72)

Zucchini Pizza
Bites (p. 73)

Cheesy Sun
Crisps (p. 62)

Cocktail Nibbles

Baked Brie with Nut Crust

⅓ cup pecans
⅓ cup almonds
⅓ cup walnuts
1 egg
1 tablespoon heavy cream
1 wheel (8 ounces) Brie cheese
2 tablespoons sugar-free raspberry jam

1. Preheat oven to 350°F. Place nuts in food processor fitted with steel blade; pulse to finely chop. *Do not overprocess.* Transfer chopped nuts to shallow dish or pie plate.

2. Combine egg and cream in another shallow dish; whisk until well blended.

3. Dip Brie into egg mixture, then into nut mixture, turning to coat. Press nuts to adhere.

4. Transfer Brie to baking sheet; spread jam over top. Bake 15 minutes or until cheese is warm and soft. *Makes 8 servings*

Maple-Glazed Meatballs

Prep Time: 10 minutes • **Cook Time:** 5 to 6 hours

1½ cups ketchup
1 cup maple syrup or maple-flavored syrup
⅓ cup reduced-sodium soy sauce
1 tablespoon quick-cooking tapioca
1½ teaspoons ground allspice
1 teaspoon dry mustard
2 packages (about 16 ounces each) frozen fully cooked meatballs, partially thawed and separated
1 can (20 ounces) pineapple chunks in juice, drained

Slow Cooker Directions

1. Combine ketchup, maple syrup, soy sauce, tapioca, allspice and mustard in slow cooker.

2. Stir meatballs and pineapple chunks into ketchup mixture.

3. Cover; cook on LOW 5 to 6 hours. Stir before serving.

Makes about 48 meatballs

Variation: Serve over hot cooked rice for an entrée.

Southwest-Spiced Walnuts

2 cups California walnuts
1 tablespoon sugar
1 teaspoon sea salt
½ teaspoon garlic powder
½ teaspoon ground cumin
¼ teaspoon cayenne pepper
1 tablespoon walnut oil

Preheat oven to 375°F. Plunge walnuts into a pot of boiling water, turn off heat and let stand 2 minutes; drain. Spread walnuts on baking sheet and roast 10 minutes. Measure seasonings in a small bowl and stir to combine. Heat oil in a skillet. Add walnuts and toss 1 minute. Add seasoning mixture and toss until walnuts are well coated. Cool on a paper towel.

Makes 2 cups

Favorite recipe from **Walnut Marketing Board**

Indian-Spiced Walnuts

2 egg whites, lightly beaten
1 tablespoon ground cumin
1½ teaspoons curry powder
1½ teaspoons salt
½ teaspoon sugar
4 cups California walnuts, halves and pieces

Preheat oven to 350°F. Coat large, shallow baking pan with nonstick cooking spray. In large bowl, mix egg whites with spices, salt and sugar. Stir in walnuts and coat thoroughly. Spread in prepared pan. Bake 15 to 18 minutes or until dry and crisp. Cool completely before serving.

Makes 4 cups

Favorite recipe from **Walnut Marketing Board**

Cheesy Sun Crisps

2 cups (8 ounces) shredded Cheddar cheese
½ cup grated Parmesan cheese
½ cup sunflower oil margarine, softened
3 tablespoons water
1 cup all-purpose flour
¼ teaspoon salt (optional)
1 cup uncooked quick oats
⅔ cup roasted, salted sunflower seeds

Beat cheeses, margarine and water in bowl until blended. Mix in flour and salt. Stir in oats and sunflower seeds until combined. Shape into 12-inch-long roll; wrap securely. Refrigerate about 4 hours or up to 1 week.

Preheat oven to 400°F. Lightly grease cookie sheets. Cut roll into slices ⅛ to ¼ inches thick; flatten each slice slightly. Place on prepared cookie sheets. Bake 8 to 10 minutes or until edges are light golden brown. Remove immediately; cool on wire rack.   *Makes 4 to 5 dozen crackers*

Favorite recipe from **National Sunflower Association**

Spiced Sesame Wonton Crisps

20 (3-inch) wonton wrappers, cut in half
1 tablespoon water
2 teaspoons olive oil
½ teaspoon paprika
½ teaspoon ground cumin or chili powder
¼ teaspoon dry mustard
1 tablespoon sesame seeds

1. Preheat oven to 375°F. Coat 2 baking sheets with nonstick cooking spray. Cut each halved wonton wrapper into 2 strips; place in single layer on prepared baking sheets.

2. Combine water, oil, paprika, cumin and mustard in small bowl; mix well. Brush oil mixture evenly onto wonton strips; sprinkle evenly with sesame seeds. Bake 6 to 8 minutes or until lightly browned. Remove to wire rack; cool completely. Transfer to serving plate.   *Makes 80 crisps*

Cocktail Wraps

16 thin strips Cheddar cheese*
16 HILLSHIRE FARM® Lit'l Smokies, scored lengthwise into halves
1 can (8 ounces) refrigerated crescent roll dough
1 egg, beaten *or* 1 tablespoon milk
Mustard

*Or substitute Swiss, taco-flavored or other variety of cheese.

Preheat oven to 400°F.

Place 1 strip cheese inside score of each Lit'l Smokie. Separate dough into 8 triangles; cut each lengthwise into halves to make 16 triangles. Place 1 link on wide end of 1 dough triangle; roll up. Repeat with remaining links and dough triangles. Place links on baking sheet. Brush dough with egg. Bake 10 to 15 minutes.

Serve hot with mustard.   *Makes 16 hors d'oeuvres*

Chili
Cashews

1 tablespoon vegetable oil
2 teaspoons chili powder
1 teaspoon ground cumin
½ teaspoon sugar
½ teaspoon red pepper flakes
2 cups roasted, salted whole cashews (about 9 ounces)

1. Preheat oven to 350°F. Line baking sheet with foil. Spray foil with nonstick cooking spray.

2. Combine oil, chili powder, cumin, sugar and red pepper in medium bowl with wire whisk. Add nuts, stirring to coat evenly. Spread onto prepared baking sheet in single layer. Bake 8 to 10 minutes or until golden, stirring once.

3. Cool completely on baking sheet. Store in airtight container.

Makes 2 cups cashews

*Tip

Serve Chili Cashews as an appetizer or a snack, or sprinkle them on salads or cottage cheese for a zesty taste treat.

Herbed Potato Chips

Nonstick olive oil cooking spray
2 medium red potatoes (about ½ pound), unpeeled
1 tablespoon olive oil
2 tablespoons minced fresh dill, thyme or rosemary *or*
    2 teaspoons dried dill weed, thyme or rosemary
¼ teaspoon garlic salt
⅛ teaspoon black pepper
1¼ cups fat-free sour cream

1. Preheat oven to 450°F. Spray baking sheets with cooking spray.

2. Cut potatoes crosswise into very thin slices, about ¹⁄₁₆ inch thick. Pat dry with paper towels. Arrange potato slices in single layer on prepared baking sheets; coat potatoes with cooking spray.

3. Bake 10 minutes; turn slices over. Brush with oil. Combine dill, garlic salt and pepper in small bowl; sprinkle evenly onto potato slices. Continue baking 5 to 10 minutes or until potatoes are golden brown. Cool on baking sheets. Serve with sour cream.   *Makes 6 servings*

Shrimp
Pâté

½ pound cooked peeled shrimp
¼ cup (½ stick) unsalted butter, cut into chunks
2 teaspoons dry vermouth or chicken broth
1 teaspoon lemon juice
1 teaspoon Dijon mustard
¼ teaspoon salt
¼ teaspoon ground mace
⅛ teaspoon ground red pepper
⅛ teaspoon black pepper
½ cup chopped pistachio nuts
2 large heads Belgian endive

1. Combine shrimp, butter, vermouth, lemon juice, mustard, salt, mace, red pepper and black pepper in blender or food processor. Process until smooth. Gently form mixture into 8-inch log on waxed paper. (If mixture is too soft to handle refrigerate 1 hour.)

2. Spread pistachio nuts on sheet of waxed paper. Roll pâté log in nuts to coat. Cover and refrigerate 1 to 3 hours.

3. Separate endive into individual leaves. Place pâté on serving plate; serve with endive leaves. *Makes 1½ cups spread*

Variation: Spoon shrimp pâté into serving bowl and sprinkle with pistachio nuts.

*Tip

Fresh seafood should have a pleasant ocean-like scent. A strong fishy or ammonia odor indicates spoilage. When buying fresh seafood, be sure to store it in the coldest part of your refrigerator and use it within 1 or 2 days.

Spicy Sweet & Sour Cocktail Franks

Prep Time: 8 minutes • **Cook Time:** 2 to 3 hours

2 packages (8 ounces each) cocktail franks
½ cup ketchup or chili sauce
½ cup apricot preserves
1 teaspoon hot pepper sauce
    Additional hot pepper sauce (optional)

Slow Cooker Directions

1. Combine all ingredients in slow cooker; mix well. Cover; cook on LOW 2 to 3 hours.

2. Serve warm or at room temperature with additional hot pepper sauce, if desired.   *Makes about 4 dozen cocktail franks*

Brie Bites

1 package (17½ ounces) frozen puff pastry, thawed
¼ cup apricot preserves or red pepper jelly
1 (5-inch) brie round, cut into 32 chunks

1. Preheat oven to 400°F. Cut each puff pastry sheet into 16 squares.

2. Spread ½ teaspoon apricot preserves on each square. Place cube of brie on one side of each square, fold over opposite edge. Use tines of fork to seal completely. Place 1 inch apart on ungreased baking sheets.

3. Bake 10 to 13 minutes or until pastry is light golden brown.

Makes 32 bites

Quick Pickled
Green Beans

½ pound (3½ cups loosely packed) whole green beans
½ red bell pepper, cut into strips (optional)
1 jalapeño* or other hot pepper, cut into strips
1 large clove garlic, cut in half
1 bay leaf
1 cup white wine vinegar
1 cup water
½ cup white wine
1 tablespoon sugar
1 tablespoon salt
1 tablespoon whole coriander seeds
1 tablespoon mustard seeds
1 tablespoon whole peppercorns

*Jalapeño peppers can sting and irritate the skin, so wear rubber gloves when handling peppers and do not touch your eyes.

1. Wash green beans; remove stem ends. Place in glass dish just large enough to hold green beans and 2½ cups liquid. Add bell pepper strips, if desired. Tuck jalapeño, garlic and bay leaf between beans.

2. Place vinegar, water, wine, sugar, salt, coriander, mustard seeds and peppercorns in medium saucepan. Heat to a boil; stir to dissolve sugar and salt. Reduce heat; simmer 5 minutes. Pour mixture over green beans, making sure beans are fully submerged in liquid. If not, add additional hot water to cover.

3. Cover; refrigerate at least 24 hours. Flavor improves in 48 hours and beans may be kept refrigerated for up to five days. Drain beans; discard bay leaf before serving. *Makes 6 servings*

Zucchini Pizza Bites

⅓ **cup salsa**
2 small zucchini, trimmed and cut diagonally into
 ¼-inch-thick slices
¼ pound chorizo sausage
6 tablespoons shredded reduced-fat mozzarella cheese

1. Preheat oven or toaster oven to 400°F. Place salsa in fine sieve and press out excess moisture; set aside to drain. Remove sausage from casing; crumble into small skillet. Cook and stir 5 minutes or until cooked through; drain fat.

2. Place zucchini on baking sheet or toaster oven tray. Spoon 1 teaspoon drained salsa on each zucchini slice. Top with chorizo, dividing evenly among zucchini slices. Sprinkle 1½ teaspoons cheese over each slice.

3. Bake 10 minutes or until cheese is lightly browned. Remove from oven and serve. *Makes 6 servings*

*Tip

Chorizo, a spicy pork sausage, is common in both Mexican and Spanish cooking. The Mexican variety (which is the kind most widely available in the U.S.) is made from raw pork while the Spanish variety is traditionally made from smoked pork. If chorizo is unavailable, substitute any variety of spicy sausage.

Herb Cheese Twists

Prep and Cook Time: 20 minutes

2 tablespoons butter or margarine
¼ cup grated Parmesan cheese
1 teaspoon dried parsley flakes
1 teaspoon dried basil
1 can (7½ ounces) refrigerated buttermilk biscuits

1. Preheat oven to 400°F. Lightly grease baking sheet. Microwave butter in small bowl on MEDIUM (50%) just until melted; cool slightly. Stir in cheese, parsley and basil. Set aside.

2. Pat each biscuit into 5×2-inch rectangle. Spread 1 teaspoon butter mixture onto each rectangle; cut each in half lengthwise. Twist each strip 3 or 4 times. Place on prepared baking sheet. Bake 8 to 10 minutes or until golden brown. *Makes 5 servings*

Variation: Save even more time by using ready-to-bake breadsticks. Spread the butter mixture onto the breadsticks, then bake them according to the package directions.

Nicole's
Cheddar Crisps

1¾ **cups all-purpose flour**
½ **cup yellow cornmeal**
¾ **teaspoon sugar**
¾ **teaspoon salt**
½ **teaspoon baking soda**
½ **cup (1 stick) butter or margarine**
1½ **cups (6 ounces) shredded sharp Cheddar cheese**
½ **cup cold water**
2 **tablespoons white vinegar**
Coarsely ground black pepper

1. Mix flour, cornmeal, sugar, salt and baking soda in large bowl. Cut in butter with pastry blender or two knives until mixture resembles coarse crumbs. Stir in cheese, water and vinegar with fork until mixture forms soft dough. Cover dough; refrigerate 1 hour or freeze 30 minutes until firm.*

2. Preheat oven to 375°F. Grease 2 cookie sheets. Divide dough into 4 pieces. Roll each piece into paper-thin circle (about 13 inches in diameter) on floured surface. Sprinkle with pepper; press pepper firmly into dough.

3. Cut each circle into 8 wedges; place on prepared cookie sheets. Bake about 10 minutes or until crisp. Store in airtight container for up to 3 days. *Makes 32 crisps*

Dough may be frozen at this point. To prepare, thaw in refrigerator and proceed as directed.

Pepper Cheese Cocktail Puffs

Prep and Bake Time: 30 minutes

½ **package frozen puff pastry dough, thawed**
1 **tablespoon Dijon mustard**
½ **cup (2 ounces) finely shredded Cheddar cheese**
1 **teaspoon cracked black pepper**
1 **egg**
1 **tablespoon water**

1. Preheat oven to 400°F. Grease baking sheets.

2. Roll out 1 sheet puff pastry dough on well floured surface to 14×10-inch rectangle. Spread half of dough (from 10-inch side) with mustard. Sprinkle with cheese and pepper. Fold dough over filling; roll gently to seal edges.

3. Cut lengthwise into 3 strips; cut each strip diagonally into 1½-inch pieces. Place on prepared baking sheets. Beat egg and water in small bowl; brush onto appetizers.

4. Bake appetizers 12 to 15 minutes or until puffed and deep golden brown. Remove from baking sheets to wire rack; cool.

Makes about 20 puffs

*Tip

Work quickly and efficiently when using puff pastry. The colder puff pastry is the better it will puff in the hot oven. This recipe can be easily doubled to use an entire package of puff pastry.

Barbecued Swedish Meatballs (p. 90)

Tortilla Pizzettes (p. 92)

Brats in Beer
(p. 100)

Cheesy Quesadillas
(p. 101)

Party Favorites

Stuffed Party Baguette

2 medium red bell peppers
1 loaf French bread (about 14 inches long)
¼ cup plus 2 tablespoons fat-free Italian dressing, divided
1 small red onion, very thinly sliced
8 large fresh basil leaves
3 ounces Swiss cheese, very thinly sliced

1. Preheat oven to 425°F. Cover large baking sheet with foil; set aside.

2. To roast bell peppers, cut peppers in half; remove stems, seeds and membranes. Place peppers, cut sides down, on prepared baking sheet. Bake 20 to 25 minutes or until skins are browned.

3. Transfer peppers from baking sheet to paper bag; close bag tightly. Let stand 10 minutes or until peppers are cool enough to handle and skins are loosened. Peel off and discard skins. Cut peppers into strips.

4. Trim ends from bread; discard. Cut loaf in half lengthwise. Remove soft insides of loaf; reserve for another use, if desired.

5. Brush ¼ cup Italian dressing evenly onto cut sides of bread. Arrange pepper strips in even layer in bottom half of loaf; top with even layer of onion. Brush onion with remaining 2 tablespoons Italian dressing; top with layer of basil and cheese. Replace bread top. Wrap loaf tightly in heavy-duty plastic wrap; refrigerate at least 2 hours or overnight.

6. When ready to serve, remove plastic wrap. Cut loaf crosswise into 1-inch slices. Secure with toothpicks and garnish, if desired.

Makes about 12 servings

Honey-Mustard Chicken Wings

Prep Time: 20 minutes • **Cook Time:** 4 to 5 hours

3 pounds chicken wings
1 teaspoon salt
1 teaspoon black pepper
½ cup honey
½ cup barbecue sauce
2 tablespoons spicy brown mustard
1 clove garlic, minced
3 to 4 thin lemon slices

Slow Cooker Directions

1. Cut off chicken wing tips; discard. Cut each wing at joint to make two pieces. Sprinkle with salt and pepper; place wing pieces on broiler rack. Broil 4 to 5 inches from heat about 10 minutes, turning halfway through cooking time. Place in slow cooker.

2. Combine honey, barbecue sauce, mustard and garlic in small bowl; mix well. Pour sauce over chicken wings. Top with lemon slices. Cover; cook on LOW 4 to 5 hours.

3. Remove and discard lemon slices. Serve wings with sauce.

Makes about 24 wings

Spinach-Artichoke Party Cups

Nonstick cooking spray
36 (3-inch) wonton wrappers
1 can (8½ ounces) artichoke hearts, drained and chopped
½ (10-ounce) package frozen chopped spinach, thawed and squeezed dry
1 cup shredded Monterey Jack cheese
½ cup grated Parmesan cheese
½ cup mayonnaise
1 clove garlic, minced

1. Preheat oven to 300°F. Spray mini (1¾-inch) muffin cups lightly with cooking spray. Press 1 wonton wrapper into each cup; spray lightly with cooking spray. Bake about 9 minutes or until light golden brown. Remove shells from pan; place on wire rack to cool. Repeat with remaining wonton wrappers.*

2. Meanwhile, combine artichoke hearts, spinach, cheeses, mayonnaise and garlic in medium bowl; mix well.

3. Fill each wonton cup with about 1½ teaspoons spinach-artichoke mixture. Place filled cups on baking sheet. Bake about 7 minutes or until heated through. Serve immediately.   *Makes 36 cups*

Wonton cups may be prepared up to one week in advance. Cool completely and store in an airtight container.

*Tip

If you have leftover spinach-artichoke mixture after filling the wonton cups, place the mixture in a shallow ovenproof dish and bake it at 350°F until hot and bubbly. Serve with bread or crackers.

Parmesan Ranch Snack Mix

Prep Time: 5 minutes • **Cook Time:** 3½ hours

3 cups corn or rice cereal squares
2 cups oyster crackers
1 package (5 ounces) bagel chips, broken in half
1½ cups mini pretzel twists
1 cup pistachio nuts
2 tablespoons grated Parmesan cheese
¼ cup (½ stick) butter, melted
1 package (1 ounce) dry ranch salad dressing mix
½ teaspoon garlic powder

Slow Cooker Directions

1. Combine cereal, oyster crackers, bagel chips, pretzels, nuts and Parmesan cheese in slow cooker; mix gently.

2. Combine butter, salad dressing mix and garlic powder in small bowl. Pour over cereal mixture; toss lightly to coat. Cover; cook on LOW 3 hours.

3. Remove cover; stir gently. Cook, uncovered, 30 minutes.

Makes about 9½ cups snack mix

Barbecued
Swedish Meatballs

Meatballs
- 1½ **pounds lean ground beef**
- 1 **cup finely chopped onion**
- ½ **cup fresh breadcrumbs**
- ½ **cup HOLLAND HOUSE® White Cooking Wine**
- 1 **egg, beaten**
- ½ **teaspoon ground allspice**
- ½ **teaspoon ground nutmeg**

Sauce
- 1 **jar (10 ounces) currant jelly**
- ½ **cup chili sauce**
- ¼ **cup HOLLAND HOUSE® White Cooking Wine**
- 1 **tablespoon cornstarch**

Heat oven to 350°F. In medium bowl, combine all meatball ingredients; mix well. Shape into 1-inch balls. Place meatballs in 15×10×1-inch baking pan. Bake 20 minutes or until brown.

In medium saucepan, combine all sauce ingredients; mix well. Cook over medium heat until mixture boils and thickens, stirring occasionally. Add meatballs. To serve, place meatballs and sauce in fondue pot or chafing dish.   *Makes 6 to 8 servings*

Dried Tomato Party Pockets

¼ cup SONOMA Dried Tomato Bits*
2 tablespoons boiling water
1 cup (4 ounces) shredded sharp Cheddar cheese
3 tablespoons sliced green onions
1 package (10 ounces) refrigerated biscuits (10 biscuits)
1 egg, beaten
2 teaspoons sesame seeds (optional)

To substitute dried tomato halves for tomato bits, measure ½ cup SONOMA Dried Tomato Halves into blender; pulse using on/off button until finely chopped.

Preheat oven to 400°F. Mix tomato bits and water in medium bowl; set aside 5 minutes. Add cheese and onions; toss to blend evenly. Roll out each biscuit to 4- to 5-inch circle on lightly floured surface. For each pocket, place about 2 tablespoons tomato mixture onto center of circle. Brush edge with egg. Fold over and press to seal completely. Place, 2 inches apart, on baking sheet. Brush with egg and sprinkle with sesame seeds, if desired. Bake 10 to 12 minutes or until golden brown. Serve warm or at room temperature. *Makes 10 (4-inch) pockets*

Piggy Wraps

1 package HILLSHIRE FARM® Lit'l Smokies
2 cans (8 ounces each) refrigerated crescent roll dough, cut into small triangles

Preheat oven to 400°F.

Wrap individual Lit'l Smokies in dough triangles. Bake 5 minutes or until golden brown. *Makes about 50 hors d'oeuvres*

Note: Piggy Wraps may be frozen. To reheat in microwave, microwave at HIGH (100% power) 1½ minutes or at MEDIUM-HIGH (70% power) 2 minutes. When reheated in microwave, dough will not be crisp.

Tortilla Pizzettes

1 cup chunky salsa
1 cup refried beans
2 tablespoons chopped fresh cilantro
½ teaspoon ground cumin
3 (10-inch) flour tortillas
1 cup (4 ounces) shredded Mexican cheese blend

1. Pour salsa into sieve; let drain at least 20 minutes.

2. Meanwhile, combine refried beans, cilantro and cumin in small bowl; mix well. Preheat oven to 400°F. Spray baking sheet lightly with nonstick cooking spray; set aside.

3. Cut each tortilla into 2½-inch circles, using round cookie cutter (9 to 10 circles per tortilla). Spread each tortilla circle with refried bean mixture, leaving ¼ inch around edge. Top each with heaping teaspoonful drained salsa; sprinkle with about 1½ teaspoons cheese.

4. Place tortillas on prepared baking sheet. Bake about 7 minutes or until tortillas are golden brown.   *Makes about 30 pizzettes*

Lit'l Party Delights

      ¾ **cup chili sauce**
      ¾ **cup grape jelly**
      4 **teaspoons red wine**
      2 **teaspoons dry mustard**
   1½ **teaspoons soy sauce**
      ½ **teaspoon ground ginger**
      ½ **teaspoon ground cinnamon**
      ½ **teaspoon ground nutmeg**
      1 **pound HILLSHIRE FARM® Lit'l Smokies**

Combine chili sauce, jelly, wine, mustard, soy sauce, ginger, cinnamon and nutmeg in medium saucepan; heat and stir over medium heat until mixture is smooth. Add Lit'l Smokies; heat 5 to 6 minutes or until hot. Serve with frilled toothpicks. *Makes about 50 hors d'oeuvres*

Taco Popcorn Olé

      9 **cups air-popped popcorn**
         Butter-flavored cooking spray
      1 **teaspoon chili powder**
      ½ **teaspoon salt**
      ½ **teaspoon garlic powder**
      ⅛ **teaspoon ground red pepper (optional)**

1. Preheat oven to 350°F. Line 15×10×1-inch jelly-roll pan with foil.

2. Place popcorn in single layer in prepared pan. Coat lightly with cooking spray.

3. Combine chili powder, salt, garlic powder and red pepper, if desired, in small bowl; sprinkle over popcorn. Mix lightly to coat evenly.

4. Bake 5 minutes or until hot, stirring gently after 3 minutes. Spread mixture in single layer on large sheet of foil to cool. Store popcorn mixture in tightly covered container at room temperature for up to 4 days. *Makes 9 cups*

Ham and Cheese "Sushi" Rolls

4 thin slices deli ham (about 4×4 inches)
1 package (8 ounces) cream cheese, softened
1 piece (4 inches long) seedless cucumber, quartered
   lengthwise (about ½ cucumber)
4 thin slices (about 4×4 inches) American or Cheddar
   cheese, at room temperature
1 red bell pepper, cut into thin 4-inch-long strips

1. For ham sushi, pat 1 ham slice with paper towel to remove excess moisture. Spread 2 tablespoons cream cheese to edges of ham slice. Pat 1 cucumber piece with paper towel to remove excess moisture; place at edge of ham slice. Roll up tightly, pressing gently to seal. Wrap in plastic wrap; refrigerate. Repeat with remaining ham slices, cream cheese and cucumber pieces.

2. For cheese sushi, spread 2 tablespoons cream cheese to edges of 1 cheese slice. Place 2 red pepper strips at edge of cheese slice. Roll up tightly, pressing gently to seal. Wrap in plastic wrap; refrigerate. Repeat with remaining cheese slices, cream cheese and red pepper strips.

3. To serve, remove plastic wrap from ham and cheese rolls. Cut each roll into 8 (½-inch-wide) pieces. *Makes 64 pieces*

Crispy Tortilla Chicken

1½ cups crushed tortilla chips
1 package (about 1 ounce) taco seasoning mix
24 chicken drummettes (about 2 pounds)
Salsa (optional)

1. Preheat oven to 350°F. Spray rimmed baking sheet with nonstick cooking spray.

2. Combine tortilla chips and taco seasoning in large shallow bowl. Coat chicken with crumb mixture, turning to coat all sides. Shake off excess crumbs; place chicken on prepared baking sheet.

3. Bake about 40 minutes or until chicken is no longer pink in center. Serve with salsa. *Makes 2 dozen drummettes*

Variation: The recipe can also be prepared using 1 pound boneless skinless chicken breasts cut into 1-inch strips. Bake at 350°F about 20 minutes or until chicken is no longer pink in center.

*Tip

This recipe could be paired with a zesty side dish for the buffet table. Cook 1 cup of white rice according to package directions, then blend in 1 can (about 16 ounces) rinsed, drained pinto beans and 1 can (about 14 ounces) drained diced tomatoes with green chiles and onions.

Brats
in Beer

Prep Time: 5 minutes • **Cook Time:** 4 to 5 hours

1½ pounds bratwurst (about 5 or 6 links)
1 bottle (12 ounces) amber ale
1 medium onion, thinly sliced
2 tablespoons packed brown sugar
2 tablespoons red wine vinegar or cider vinegar
  Spicy brown mustard
  Cocktail rye bread

Slow Cooker Directions

1. Combine bratwurst, ale, onion, brown sugar and vinegar in slow cooker. Cover; cook on LOW 4 to 5 hours.

2. Remove bratwurst and onion slices from slow cooker. Cut bratwurst into ½-inch-thick slices. For mini open-faced sandwiches, spread mustard on cocktail rye bread. Top with bratwurst slices and cooked onion.

Makes 30 to 36 appetizers

*Tip

Choose a light-tasting beer for cooking brats. Hearty ales might leave the meat tasting slightly bitter.

Cheesy Quesadillas

Prep Time: 10 minutes • **Cook Time:** 15 minutes

½ **pound ground beef**
1 **medium onion, chopped**
¼ **teaspoon salt**
1 **can (4½ ounces) chopped green chilies, drained**
1 **jar (1 pound 10 ounces) RAGÚ® Robusto!® Pasta Sauce**
8 **(6½-inch) flour tortillas**
1 **tablespoon olive oil**
2 **cups shredded Cheddar and/or mozzarella cheese
    (about 8 ounces)**

1. Preheat oven to 400°F. In 12-inch skillet, brown ground beef with onion and salt over medium-high heat; drain. Stir in chilies and ½ cup Ragú Pasta Sauce; set aside.

2. Meanwhile, evenly brush one side of 4 tortillas with half of the olive oil. On cookie sheets, arrange tortillas, oil-side down. Evenly top with ½ of the cheese, beef filling, then remaining cheese. Top with remaining 4 tortillas, then brush tops with remaining oil.

3. Bake 10 minutes or until cheese is melted. To serve, cut each quesadilla into 4 wedges. Serve with remaining sauce, heated.   *Makes 4 servings*

Toasted Pesto Rounds

¼ **cup thinly sliced fresh basil or chopped fresh dill**
¼ **cup grated Parmesan cheese**
3 **tablespoons reduced-fat mayonnaise**
1 **medium clove garlic, minced**
12 **French bread slices, about ¼ inch thick**
1 **tablespoon plus 1 teaspoon chopped fresh tomato**
1 **green onion with top, sliced**
   Black pepper

1. Preheat broiler.

2. Combine basil, cheese, mayonnaise and garlic in small bowl; mix well.

3. Arrange bread slices in single layer on ungreased nonstick baking sheet or broiler pan. Broil 6 to 8 inches from heat 30 to 45 seconds or until bread slices are lightly toasted.

4. Turn bread slices over; spread evenly with basil mixture. Broil 1 minute or until lightly browned. Top evenly with tomato and green onion. Season to taste with pepper. Transfer to serving plate. *Makes 12 servings*

Hearty Nachos

Prep Time: 10 minutes • **Cook Time:** 12 minutes

1 pound ground beef
1 envelope LIPTON® RECIPE SECRETS® Onion Soup Mix
1 can (19 ounces) black beans, rinsed and drained
1 cup salsa
1 package (8½ ounces) plain tortilla chips
1 cup shredded Cheddar cheese (about 4 ounces)

1. In 12-inch nonstick skillet, brown ground beef over medium-high heat; drain.

2. Stir in soup mix, black beans and salsa. Bring to a boil over high heat. Reduce heat to low and simmer 5 minutes or until heated through.

3. Arrange tortilla chips on serving platter. Spread beef mixture over chips; sprinkle with Cheddar cheese. Top, if desired, with sliced green onions, sliced pitted ripe olives, chopped tomato and chopped cilantro.

Makes 8 servings

*Tip

This is an ideal recipe to make when you're short on time. If you can, arrange the chips and chop the topping ingredients the night before your party, then cook the beef and assemble the nachos just before your guests arrive.

**Greek-Style Grilled
Feta (p. 118)**

**Chicken Parmesan
Stromboli (p. 115)**

Mexican Roll-Ups
(p. 124)

Easy Sausage Empanadas
(p. 114)

Ethnic Eats

Crab Cakes
Canton

**7 ounces thawed frozen cooked crabmeat or imitation
  crabmeat, drained and flaked**
1½ cups fresh whole wheat bread crumbs (about 3 slices)
¼ cup thinly sliced green onions
1 clove garlic, minced
1 teaspoon minced fresh ginger
2 egg whites, lightly beaten
1 tablespoon teriyaki sauce
2 teaspoons vegetable oil, divided
  Prepared sweet and sour sauce (optional)

1. Combine crabmeat, bread crumbs, onions, garlic and ginger in medium bowl; mix well. Add egg whites and teriyaki sauce; mix well. Shape into patties about ½ inch thick and 2 inches in diameter.*

2. Heat 1 teaspoon oil in large nonstick skillet over medium heat until hot. Add about half of crab cakes to skillet. Cook 2 minutes per side or until golden brown. Remove to serving plate; keep warm. Repeat with remaining 1 teaspoon oil and crab cakes. Serve with sweet and sour sauce, if desired. *Makes 12 cakes*

Crab cakes may be made ahead to this point; cover and refrigerate up to 24 hours before cooking.

Asian Vegetable Rolls with Soy-Lime Dipping Sauce

Prep Time: 15 minutes

¼ **cup reduced-sodium soy sauce**
2 **tablespoons lime juice**
1 **teaspoon honey**
1 **clove garlic, crushed**
½ **teaspoon finely chopped fresh ginger**
¼ **teaspoon dark sesame oil**
⅛ **to** ¼ **teaspoon red pepper flakes**
½ **cup grated cucumber**
⅓ **cup grated carrot**
¼ **cup sliced yellow bell pepper**
2 **tablespoons thinly sliced green onion**
18 **small lettuce leaves**
   Sesame seeds (optional)

1. Combine soy sauce, lime juice, honey, garlic, ginger, oil and pepper flakes in small bowl.

2. Combine cucumber, carrot, bell pepper and green onion in medium bowl.

3. Add 1 tablespoon soy sauce mixture to vegetable mixture; stir until blended. Place about 1 tablespoon vegetable mixture on each lettuce leaf. Roll up leaves; top with sesame seeds at time of serving. Serve with remaining sauce.

Makes 18 rolls

Easy Cheese Fondue

1 pound low-sodium Swiss cheese (Gruyère, Emmentaler or combination of both), shredded or cubed
2 tablespoons cornstarch
1 clove garlic, minced
1 cup HOLLAND HOUSE® White or White with Lemon Cooking Wine
1 tablespoon kirsch or cherry brandy (optional)
Pinch nutmeg
Ground black pepper

1. In medium bowl, coat cheese with cornstarch; set aside. Rub inside of ceramic fondue pot or heavy saucepan with garlic; discard garlic. Bring wine to gentle simmer over medium heat. Gradually stir in cheese to ensure smooth fondue. Once smooth, stir in brandy, if desired. Garnish with nutmeg and pepper.

2. Serve with bite-sized chunks of French bread, broccoli, cauliflower, tart apples or pears. Spear with fondue forks or wooden skewers.

Makes 1¼ cups fondue

Zesty Bruschetta

1 envelope LIPTON® RECIPE SECRETS® Savory Herb with Garlic Soup Mix
6 tablespoons BERTOLLI® Olive Oil*
1 loaf French or Italian bread (about 18 inches long), sliced lengthwise
2 tablespoons shredded or grated Parmesan cheese

*Substitution: Use ½ cup margarine or butter, melted.

1. Preheat oven to 350°F. Blend soup mix and oil. Brush onto bread, then sprinkle with cheese.

2. Bake 12 minutes or until golden. Slice, then serve.

Makes 1 loaf, about 18 pieces

Easy Sausage Empanadas

Prep Time: 25 minutes • **Cook Time:** 15 minutes

¼ **pound bulk pork sausage**
1 **(15-ounce) package refrigerated pie crusts (2 crusts)**
2 **tablespoons finely chopped onion**
⅛ **teaspoon garlic powder**
⅛ **teaspoon ground cumin**
⅛ **teaspoon dried oregano**
1 **tablespoon chopped pimiento-stuffed olives**
1 **tablespoon chopped raisins**
1 **egg, separated**

Let pie crusts stand at room temperature for 20 minutes or according to package directions. Crumble sausage into medium skillet. Add onion, garlic powder, cumin and oregano; cook over medium-high heat until sausage is no longer pink. Drain drippings. Stir in olives and raisins. Beat egg yolk slightly; stir into sausage mixture, mixing well. Carefully unfold crusts. Cut into desired shapes using 3-inch cookie cutters. Place about 2 teaspoons sausage filling on half the cutouts. Top with remaining cutouts. (Or, use round cutter, top with sausage filling and fold dough over to create half-moon shape.) Moisten fingers with water and pinch dough to seal edges. Slightly beat egg white; gently brush over tops of empanadas. Bake in 425°F oven 15 to 18 minutes or until golden brown.

Makes 12 appetizer servings

Favorite recipe from **National Pork Board**

Chicken Parmesan Stromboli

1 pound boneless, skinless chicken breast halves
½ teaspoon salt
¼ teaspoon ground black pepper
2 teaspoons olive oil
2 cups shredded mozzarella cheese (about 8 ounces)
1 jar (1 pound 10 ounces) RAGÚ® Chunky Pasta Sauce, divided
2 tablespoons grated Parmesan cheese
1 tablespoon finely chopped fresh parsley
1 pound fresh or thawed frozen bread dough

Preheat oven to 400°F. Season chicken with salt and pepper. In 12-inch skillet, heat olive oil over medium-high heat and brown chicken. Remove chicken from skillet and let cool; pull into large shreds.

In medium bowl, combine chicken, mozzarella cheese, ½ cup Ragú Chunky Pasta Sauce, Parmesan cheese and parsley; set aside.

On greased jelly-roll pan, press dough to form 12×10-inch rectangle. Arrange chicken mixture down center of dough. Cover filling bringing one long side into center, then overlap with the other long side; pinch seam to seal. Fold in ends and pinch to seal. Arrange on pan, seam-side down. Gently press in sides to form 12×4-inch loaf. Bake 35 minutes or until dough is cooked and golden. Cut stromboli into slices. Heat remaining pasta sauce and serve with stromboli.   *Makes 6 servings*

Spanish-Style Garlic Shrimp

4 tablespoons I CAN'T BELIEVE IT'S NOT BUTTER!® Spread, divided
1 pound uncooked medium shrimp, peeled and deveined
½ teaspoon salt
2 cloves garlic, finely chopped
½ to 1 jalapeño pepper, seeded and finely chopped
¼ cup chopped fresh cilantro or parsley
1 tablespoon fresh lime juice

In 12-inch nonstick skillet, melt 1 tablespoon I Can't Believe It's Not Butter!® Spread over high heat and cook shrimp with salt 2 minutes or until shrimp are almost pink, turning once. Remove shrimp and set aside.

In same skillet, melt remaining 3 tablespoons I Can't Believe It's Not Butter!® Spread over medium-low heat and cook garlic and jalapeño pepper, stirring occasionally, 1 minute. Return shrimp to skillet. Stir in cilantro and lime juice and heat 30 seconds or until shrimp turn pink. Serve, if desired, with crusty Italian bread.   *Makes 6 servings*

*Tip

In Spain, garlic shrimp is a popular tapas dish. Tapas are traditionally bar snacks—small plates of something tasty to accompany drinks. They often include olives, omelets, seafood and roasted peppers.

Greek-Style Grilled Feta

1 package (8 ounces) feta cheese, sliced in half horizontally
24 (¼-inch-thick) slices small onion
½ green bell pepper, thinly sliced
½ red bell pepper, thinly sliced
½ teaspoon dried oregano
¼ teaspoon garlic pepper or black pepper
24 (½-inch-thick) slices French bread

1. Spray 14-inch-long sheet of foil with nonstick cooking spray. Cut feta into 24 slices. Place onion slices in center of foil and top with feta slices. Sprinkle with bell pepper slices, oregano and garlic pepper. Bring the two long sides of foil together above the food; fold down in a series of locked folds, allowing for heat circulation and expansion. Fold the short ends up and over again. Press folds firmly to seal the foil packet.

2. Prepare grill for direct grilling. Place foil packet on grid; grill, covered, over hot coals 15 minutes. Turn packet over; grill, covered, 15 minutes more.

3. Open packet carefully. Serve immediately with slices of French bread.

Makes 24 appetizers

*Tip

Fresh feta cheese is available in slices immersed in brine, usually at your grocer's deli counter. If you buy feta this way, make sure to store it tightly covered or it will dry out very quickly. If you have leftover feta, try crumbling it into a salad or on pizza.

Pepperoni-Oregano Focaccia

1 tablespoon cornmeal
1 package (10 ounces) refrigerated pizza crust dough
½ cup finely chopped pepperoni (3 to 3½ ounces)
1½ teaspoons finely chopped fresh oregano *or* ½ teaspoon dried oregano
2 teaspoons extra-virgin olive oil

1. Preheat oven to 425°F. Spray baking sheet with nonstick cooking spray; sprinkle with cornmeal. Set aside.

2. Unroll dough onto lightly floured surface. Pat dough into 12×9-inch rectangle. Sprinkle half the pepperoni and half the oregano over one side of dough. Fold over dough, making 12×4½-inch rectangle.

3. Roll dough into 12×9-inch rectangle. Place on prepared baking sheet. Prick dough with fork at 2-inch intervals about 30 times. Brush with oil; sprinkle with remaining pepperoni and oregano.

4. Bake 12 to 15 minutes or until golden brown. Prick dough several more times during baking if dough puffs up. Cut into strips.

Makes 12 servings

Fried
Calamari

**1 pound cleaned squid (body tubes, tentacles or a
    combination)**
¾ cup fine dry bread crumbs
1 egg
1 tablespoon milk
  Vegetable oil
  Prepared tartar sauce
  Lemon wedges (optional)

1. Rinse squid under cold running water. Cut each squid body tube crosswise into ¼-inch rings. Pat pieces thoroughly dry with paper towels.

2. Spread bread crumbs on plate. Beat egg with milk in medium bowl. Add squid pieces; stir to coat well. Dip squid pieces in bread crumbs; place in shallow bowl or on waxed paper. Let stand 10 to 15 minutes before frying.

3. To deep fry squid, heat 1½ inches oil in large saucepan to 350°F. (Caution: Squid will pop and spatter during frying; do not stand too close to pan.) Fry 8 to 10 pieces of squid at a time without crowding 45 to 60 seconds until light brown.* Adjust heat to maintain temperature. Remove with slotted spoon; drain on paper towels. Repeat with remaining squid pieces. *Do not overcook squid or it will become tough.*

4. Serve hot with Tartar Sauce and lemon wedges.

Makes 2 to 3 servings

*To shallow fry squid, heat about ¼ inch oil in large skillet over medium-high heat; reduce heat to medium. Add single layer of squid to oil without crowding. Cook 1 minute per side or until light brown. Proceed as directed in step 3.

Mexican Roll-Ups

2 packages (3 ounces each) cream cheese, softened
¾ cup sour cream
1 package (15.2 ounces) ORTEGA® Soft Taco Kit
1 can (4 ounces) ORTEGA Diced Green Chiles, drained
¾ cup finely shredded Cheddar cheese
20 (2½×⅜-inch) roasted red pepper strips

BEAT together cream cheese, sour cream and seasoning mix from Soft Taco Kit until smooth. Stir in green chiles and Cheddar cheese.

SPREAD 3 tablespoons cream cheese mixture evenly over each tortilla from kit. Place 2 red pepper strips in center of each tortilla; roll up and wrap in plastic wrap.

CHILL at least 3 hours.

CUT each roll-up into 7 (¾-inch) slices.

SERVE with taco sauce from kit for dipping.   *Makes 70 roll-ups*

Note: Roasted red pepper strips can be purchased in 16-ounce jars in the condiment section at most supermarkets.

Thai Satay Chicken Skewers

1 pound boneless skinless chicken breasts
⅓ cup soy sauce
2 tablespoons fresh lime juice
2 cloves garlic, minced
1 teaspoon grated fresh ginger
¾ teaspoon red pepper flakes
2 tablespoons water
¾ cup canned unsweetened coconut milk
1 tablespoon creamy peanut butter
4 green onions cut into 1-inch pieces

1. Cut chicken crosswise into ⅜-inch-wide strips; place in shallow glass dish. Combine soy sauce, lime juice, garlic, ginger and red pepper flakes in small bowl; reserve 3 tablespoons. Add water to remaining mixture. Pour over chicken; toss to coat well. Cover; marinate in refrigerator at least 30 minutes or up to 2 hours, stirring occasionally.

2. Soak 8 (10- to 12-inch) bamboo skewers 20 minutes in cold water to prevent them from burning; drain. Prepare grill for direct cooking.

3. Meanwhile, for peanut sauce, combine coconut milk, reserved soy sauce mixture and peanut butter in small saucepan. Bring to a boil over medium-high heat, stirring constantly. Reduce heat and simmer, uncovered, 2 to 4 minutes or until sauce thickens. Keep warm.

4. Drain chicken; reserve marinade. Weave 3 to 4 chicken strips accordion-style onto each skewer, alternating with green onion pieces. Brush chicken and onions with reserved marinade. Discard remaining marinade.

5. Place skewers on grid. Grill skewers, uncovered, over medium-hot coals 6 to 8 minutes or until chicken is cooked through, turning halfway through grilling time. Serve with warm peanut sauce for dipping.

Makes 4 skewers

Marinated Antipasto

6 cups water, divided
1 cup matchstick-size carrot pieces
1 cup fresh green beans, cut into 2-inch pieces
1 cup fresh brussels sprouts, quartered
1 cup thinly sliced baby yellow squash
½ cup thinly sliced red bell pepper
½ cup thinly sliced yellow bell pepper
1 can (9 ounces) artichoke hearts, drained and quartered
½ cup white wine vinegar
1 tablespoon olive oil
1 teaspoon sugar
2 bay leaves
1 clove garlic
6 sprigs fresh thyme
¼ teaspoon black pepper
½ cup chopped green onions
½ cup minced fresh parsley
    Peel of 2 oranges, cut into thin strips

1. Bring 4 cups water to a boil in large saucepan over high heat. Add carrots, beans and brussels sprouts; cover and simmer 1 minute. Add squash and bell peppers; cover and simmer 1 minute or until vegetables are crisp-tender. Remove from heat; drain. Place vegetables and artichoke hearts in heatproof bowl.

2. Combine remaining 2 cups water, vinegar, oil, sugar, bay leaves, garlic, thyme and black pepper in medium saucepan. Bring to a boil over medium heat. Pour over vegetables; mix well. Cool completely. Cover and refrigerate 12 hours or up to 3 days before serving.

3. Before serving, drain vegetables. Discard bay leaves, garlic and thyme. Toss vegetables with green onions, parsley and orange peel.

Makes 8 servings

Shrimp
Toast

12 large shrimp, shelled and deveined, tails intact
1 egg
2 tablespoons plus 1½ teaspoons cornstarch
¼ teaspoon salt
Dash black pepper
3 slices white sandwich bread, crusts removed, quartered
1 hard-cooked egg yolk, cut into ½-inch pieces
1 slice (1 ounce) cooked ham, cut into ½-inch pieces
1 green onion, finely chopped
Vegetable oil for frying

1. Cut deep slit down back of each shrimp; press gently with fingers to flatten.

2. Beat egg, cornstarch, salt and pepper in large bowl until blended. Add shrimp; toss to coat well.

3. Drain each shrimp and press, cut side down, into each piece of bread. Brush small amount of leftover egg mixture onto each shrimp.

4. Place one piece each of egg yolk and ham and scant ¼ teaspoon green onion on top of each shrimp.

5. Heat about 1 inch oil in wok or large skillet over medium-high heat to 375°F. Add three or four bread pieces at a time; cook 1 to 2 minutes, then spoon hot oil over shrimp toasts until shrimp is cooked through and toast is golden brown. Drain on paper towels. *Makes 12 appetizers*

Key Lime Tartlets
(p. 144)

Reese's® Haystacks
(p. 143)

Pineapple Fruit Tart
(p. 142)

Snowball Bites
(p. 151)

Sweet Treats

White Chocolate-Dipped Apricots

3 ounces white chocolate, coarsely chopped
20 dried apricot halves

1. Line baking sheet with waxed paper; set aside. Melt white chocolate in bowl over simmering water, stirring constantly.

2. Dip half of each apricot piece in chocolate, coating both sides. Place on prepared baking sheet. Refrigerate until firm. Store in refrigerator in airtight container between layers of waxed paper.   *Makes 20 apricots*

Stuffed Pecans

½ cup semisweet chocolate chips
¼ cup sweetened condensed milk
½ teaspoon vanilla
½ cup powdered sugar
80 large pecan halves

Melt chocolate chips in small saucepan over very low heat, stirring constantly. Remove from heat. Stir in sweetened condensed milk and vanilla until smooth. Stir in powdered sugar to make stiff mixture. (If chocolate mixture is too soft, refrigerate until easier to handle.)

Place 1 rounded teaspoonful chocolate mixture on flat side of 1 pecan half. Top with another pecan half. Repeat with remaining chocolate mixture and pecans. Store in refrigerator.   *Makes about 40 candies*

Dessert Grape Clusters

2 pounds seedless red and/or green grapes
1 pound premium white chocolate, coarsely chopped
2 cups finely chopped honey-roasted cashews

1. Rinse grapes under cold running water in colander; drain well. Cut grapes into clusters of 3 grapes. Place clusters in single layer on paper towels. Let stand at room temperature until completely dry.

2. Melt white chocolate in bowl over simmering water. Stir until white chocolate is melted. Remove from heat.

3. Place cashews in shallow bowl. Working with 1 cluster at a time, holding by stem, dip grapes into melted chocolate. Allow excess to drain back into bowl. Roll grapes gently in cashews. Place grapes, stem sides up, on waxed paper; repeat with remaining clusters. Refrigerate until firm. Serve within 4 hours. *Makes about 3 dozen clusters*

Easy Microwave Fudge

3¾ cups powdered sugar
½ cup unsweetened cocoa powder
¼ cup evaporated milk
2 teaspoons vanilla
½ cup butter or margarine, cut into pieces
¾ cup chopped pecans

1. Line 8-inch square pan with buttered foil; set aside.

2. Sift powdered sugar and cocoa into 2-quart microwavable bowl. Stir in milk and vanilla. Top with butter. Microwave on HIGH 3 minutes or until butter melts and mixture is hot.

3. Stir in pecans. Spread into prepared pan. Refrigerate until firm.

4. Remove fudge from pan by lifting out foil. Cut into squares. Store in refrigerator. *Makes about 1½ pounds*

Easy Egg Nog Pound Cake

Prep Time: 10 minutes • **Bake Time:** 40 to 45 minutes

1 (18.25-ounce) package yellow cake mix
1 (4-serving size) package instant vanilla pudding and pie filling mix
¾ cup BORDEN® EggNog
¾ cup vegetable oil
4 eggs
½ teaspoon ground nutmeg
Confectioners' sugar (optional)

1. Preheat oven to 350°F. In large bowl, combine cake mix, pudding mix, BORDEN® EggNog and oil; beat on low speed until moistened. Add eggs and nutmeg; beat at medium-high speed 4 minutes.

2. Pour into greased and floured 10-inch fluted or tube pan. Bake 40 to 45 minutes or until toothpick inserted near center comes out clean. Cool 10 minutes; remove from pan. Cool completely. Sprinkle with confectioners' sugar (optional). *Makes one (10-inch) cake*

*Tip

Fluted tube pans or bundt pans come in many different shapes, from sunflowers to cascading waves to castles. Make sure you grease all areas of the pan well, paying special attention to grooves.

Lemon-Orange Party Cake

1 package (18¼ ounces) yellow cake mix with pudding in the mix
1¼ cups plus 5 tablespoons orange juice, divided
3 eggs
⅓ cup vegetable oil
2 tablespoons grated orange peel
5½ cups sifted powdered sugar, divided
⅓ cup lemon juice
⅓ cup butter, softened
Multi-colored sprinkles
20 jellied orange or lemon slices

1. Preheat oven to 350°F. Lightly grease 13×9-inch baking pan.

2. Beat cake mix, 1¼ cups orange juice, eggs, oil and orange peel in large bowl with electric mixer at low speed about 1 minute or until blended. Increase speed to medium; beat 1 to 2 minutes or until smooth. Spread in prepared pan.

3. Bake 33 to 38 minutes or until toothpick inserted into center comes out clean. Meanwhile, combine 1 cup powdered sugar and lemon juice in small bowl; stir until smooth.

4. Pierce top of warm cake generously with large fork or wooden skewer at ½-inch intervals. Slowly drizzle lemon glaze over warm cake. Cool completely.

5. Beat remaining 4½ cups powdered sugar and butter in large bowl with electric mixer at low speed until blended. Beat in enough remaining orange juice to reach spreading consistency. Spread frosting over cooled cake. Decorate top of cake with sprinkles and candied fruit slices.

Makes 20 servings

Fluted Kisses® Cups with Peanut Butter Filling

72 HERSHEY'S KISSES® Brand Milk Chocolates, divided
1 cup REESE'S® Creamy Peanut Butter
1 cup powdered sugar
1 tablespoon butter or margarine, softened

1. Line small baking cups (1¾ inches in diameter) with small paper bake cups. Remove wrappers from chocolates.

2. Place 48 chocolates in small microwave-safe bowl. Microwave at HIGH (100%) 1 minute or until chocolate is melted and smooth when stirred. Using small brush, coat inside of paper cups with melted chocolate.

3. Refrigerate 20 minutes; reapply melted chocolate to any thin spots. Refrigerate until firm, preferably overnight. Gently peel paper from chocolate cups.

4. Beat peanut butter, powdered sugar and butter with electric mixer on medium speed in small bowl until smooth. Spoon into chocolate cups. Before serving, top each cup with a chocolate piece. Cover; store cups in refrigerator. *Makes about 2 dozen pieces*

Pineapple Fruit Tart

¼ **cup ground almonds (about 2 tablespoons whole almonds)**
¼ **cup butter or margarine, softened**
¼ **cup sugar**
2 **tablespoons milk**
½ **teaspoon almond extract**
¾ **cup all-purpose flour**
2 **packages (3 ounces each) cream cheese, softened**
2 **tablespoons sour cream**
¼ **cup apricot preserves, divided**
1 **teaspoon vanilla extract**
1 **can (15¼ ounces) DEL MONTE® Sliced Pineapple In Its Own Juice, drained and cut in halves**
2 **kiwifruits, peeled, sliced and cut into halves**
1 **cup sliced strawberries**

1. Combine almonds, butter, sugar, milk and almond extract; mix well. Blend in flour. Chill dough 1 hour.

2. Press dough evenly onto bottom and up side of tart pan with removable bottom.

3. Bake at 350°F, 15 to 18 minutes or until golden brown. Cool.

4. Combine cream cheese, sour cream, 1 tablespoon apricot preserves and vanilla. Spread onto crust. Arrange pineapple, kiwi and strawberries over cream cheese mixture.

5. Heat remaining 3 tablespoons apricot preserves in small saucepan over low heat. Spoon over fruit. *Makes 8 servings*

Reese's®
Haystacks

1⅔ cups (10-ounce package) REESE'S® Peanut Butter Chips
1 tablespoon shortening (do *not* use butter, margarine, spread or oil)
2½ cups (5-ounce can) chow mein noodles

1. Line tray with wax paper.

2. Place peanut butter chips and shortening in medium microwave-safe bowl. Microwave at HIGH (100%) 1 minute; stir. If necessary, microwave at HIGH an additional 15 seconds at a time, stirring after each heating, just until chips are melted and mixture is smooth when stirred. Immediately add chow mein noodles; stir to coat.

3. Drop mixture by heaping teaspoons onto prepared tray or into paper candy cups. Let stand until firm. If necessary, cover and refrigerate several minutes until firm. Store in tightly covered container.

Makes about 2 dozen treats

Honey Strawberry Tart

⅓ cup honey
1 tablespoon lemon juice
1 baked or ready-to-eat 9-inch pie shell
4 cups halved fresh strawberries
Mint sprigs for garnish (optional)

Combine honey and lemon juice in small bowl; mix well. Brush bottom of pie shell with mixture. Fill shell with strawberries. Drizzle remaining honey mixture over berries. Garnish with mint sprigs, if desired.

Makes 8 servings

Tip: Prepare honey glaze and strawberries. Fill shell and glaze strawberries just before serving to prevent shell from becoming soggy.

Favorite recipe from **National Honey Board**

Key Lime
Tartlets

1 package (18 ounces) refrigerated sugar cookie dough
½ cup finely chopped pecans
1 can (14 ounces) sweetened condensed milk
¼ cup plus 1 tablespoon bottled key lime juice
1 teaspoon freshly grated lime peel
   Whipped cream, additional freshly grated lime peel and
   lime wedge candies

1. Preheat oven to 350°F. Lightly grease 18 standard (2½-inch) muffin cups or line with paper or foil baking cups. Let dough stand at room temperature about 15 minutes.

2. Combine dough and pecans in large bowl; beat until well blended. Shape dough into 18 balls; press onto bottoms and up sides of prepared muffin cups.

3. Bake 12 to 15 minutes or until set. Remove from oven; gently press down center of each cookie cup with back of teaspoon. Cool in pan 10 minutes. Remove cups from pans; cool completely on wire rack.

4. Combine sweetened condensed milk, juice and peel in small bowl; stir until well blended. Divide evenly among cookie cups. Garnish with whipped cream, lime peel and lime candies.   *Makes 18 tartlets*

Party Mints

Prep Time: 30 minutes • **Stand Time:** 8 hours

1 (14-ounce) can EAGLE BRAND® Sweetened Condensed Milk (NOT evaporated milk)
1 (32-ounce) package confectioners' sugar
½ teaspoon peppermint extract
Assorted colored granulated sugar or crystals

1. In medium bowl, beat EAGLE BRAND® and half of confectioners' sugar until blended. Gradually add remaining confectioners' sugar and peppermint extract, beating until stiff.

2. Shape mixture into ½-inch balls. Roll in desired sugar; place on parchment paper. Let stand 8 hours to set. Store covered at room temperature. *Makes 3 dozen mints*

Variation: You many also dip uncoated mints in melted bittersweet chocolate for a different flavor.

Libby's® Famous Pumpkin Pie

- ¾ **cup granulated sugar**
- 1 **teaspoon ground cinnamon**
- ½ **teaspoon salt**
- ½ **teaspoon ground ginger**
- ¼ **teaspoon ground cloves**
- 2 **large eggs**
- 1 **can (15 ounces) LIBBY'S® 100% Pure Pumpkin**
- 1 **can (12 fluid ounces) NESTLÉ® CARNATION® Evaporated Milk**
- 1 *unbaked* **9-inch (4-cup volume) deep-dish pie shell**
  Whipped cream

MIX sugar, cinnamon, salt, ginger and cloves in small bowl. Beat eggs in large bowl. Stir in pumpkin and sugar-spice mixture. Gradually stir in evaporated milk.

POUR into pie shell.

BAKE in preheated 425°F. oven for 15 minutes. Reduce temperature to 350°F.; bake for 40 to 50 minutes or until knife inserted near center comes out clean. Cool on wire rack for 2 hours. Serve immediately or refrigerate. Top with whipped cream before serving.   *Makes 8 servings*

Note: Do not freeze, as this will cause the crust to separate from the filling.

Tip: 1¾ teaspoons pumpkin pie spice may be substituted for the cinnamon, ginger and cloves; however, the taste will be slightly different.

For 2 shallow pies: Substitute two 9-inch (2-cup volume) pie shells. Bake in preheated 425°F. oven for 15 minutes. Reduce temperature to 350°F.; bake for 20 to 30 minutes or until pies test done.

Oats 'n' Apple Tart

1½ cups uncooked quick oats
½ cup packed brown sugar, divided
1 tablespoon plus ¼ teaspoon ground cinnamon, divided
5 tablespoons butter or margarine, melted
2 medium sweet apples, such as Golden Delicious, unpeeled, cored and thinly sliced
1 teaspoon lemon juice
¼ cup water
1 envelope unflavored gelatin
½ cup apple juice concentrate
1 package (8 ounces) reduced-fat cream cheese, softened
⅛ teaspoon ground nutmeg

1. Preheat oven to 350°F. Combine oats, ¼ cup brown sugar and 1 tablespoon cinnamon in medium bowl. Add butter and stir until combined. Press onto bottom and up side of 9-inch pie plate. Bake 7 minutes or until set. Cool on wire rack.

2. Toss apple slices with lemon juice in small bowl; set aside. Place water in small saucepan. Sprinkle gelatin over water; let stand 3 to 5 minutes. Stir in apple juice concentrate. Cook and stir over medium heat until gelatin is dissolved. *Do not boil.* Remove from heat and set aside.

3. Beat cream cheese in medium bowl with electric mixer at medium speed until fluffy and smooth. Add remaining ¼ cup brown sugar, ¼ teaspoon cinnamon and nutmeg. Mix until smooth. Slowly beat in gelatin mixture on low speed until blended and creamy, about 1 minute. *Do not overbeat.*

4. Arrange apple slices in crust. Pour cream cheese mixture evenly over top. Refrigerate 2 hours or until set. *Makes 8 servings*

Snowball Bites

1 package (18 ounces) refrigerated sugar cookie dough
¾ cup all-purpose flour
2 tablespoons honey or maple syrup
1 cup chopped walnuts or pecans
Powdered sugar

1. Let dough stand at room temperature about 15 minutes.

2. Beat dough, flour and honey in large bowl with electric mixer at medium speed until well blended. Stir in walnuts. Shape dough into disk; wrap tightly in plastic wrap. Refrigerate dough at least 2 hours or up to 2 days.

3. Preheat oven to 350°F. Place powdered sugar in small bowl; set aside. Shape dough into ¾-inch balls; place 1½ inches apart on ungreased cookie sheets.

4. Bake 10 to 12 minutes or until bottoms are browned. Roll warm cookies in powdered sugar. Cool completely on wire racks. Just before serving, roll cookies in additional powdered sugar, if desired.

Makes about 2½ dozen cookies

*Tip

For a different flavor, try mixing mini chocolate chips or chopped dried fruit into the dough in addition to, or instead of, the nuts. You can also add 1 teaspoon of unsweetened cocoa powder to the powdered sugar for dusting for a more complex taste.

Cocoa Nut Bundles

1 can (8 ounces) refrigerated quick crescent dinner rolls
2 tablespoons butter or margarine, softened
1 tablespoon granulated sugar
2 teaspoons HERSHEY'S Cocoa
¼ cup chopped nuts
    Powdered sugar (optional)

1. Heat oven to 375°F. Unroll dough on ungreased cookie sheet and separate to form 8 triangles.

2. Combine butter, granulated sugar and cocoa in small bowl. Add nuts; mix thoroughly. Divide chocolate mixture evenly among triangles, placing on wide end of triangle. Take dough on either side of mixture and pull up and over mixture, tucking ends under. Continue rolling dough toward opposite point.

3. Bake 9 to 10 minutes or until golden brown. Sprinkle with powdered sugar, if desired; serve warm.   *Makes 8 rolls*

Creamy Chocolate Tarts

⅔ cup **HERSHEY'S Semi-Sweet Chocolate Chips**
¼ cup **milk**
 1 tablespoon **sugar**
½ teaspoon **vanilla extract**
½ cup **chilled whipping cream**
 6 (one 4-ounce package) **single-serve graham crusts**
   Sweetened whipped cream
   Sliced fresh fruit, maraschino cherries, chilled cherry pie filling or fresh mint

1. Place chocolate chips, milk and sugar in small microwave-safe bowl. Microwave at HIGH (100%) 1 minute or until milk is hot and chips are melted when stirred. With wire whisk or rotary beater beat until mixture is smooth; stir in vanilla. Cool to room temperature.

2. Beat whipping cream until stiff; carefully fold chocolate mixture into whipped cream until blended. Spoon or pipe into crusts. Cover; refrigerate until set. Top with sweetened whipped cream. Garnish as desired. *Makes 6 servings*

The publisher would like to thank the companies and organizations listed below for the use of their recipes and photographs in this publication.

Bob Evans®

Cabot® Creamery Cooperative

Del Monte Corporation

EAGLE BRAND®

Guiltless Gourmet®

The Hershey Company

Hillshire Farm®

Holland House® is a registered trademark of Mott's, LLP

National Cattlemen's Beef Association on Behalf of The Beef Checkoff

National Honey Board

National Pork Board

National Sunflower Association

Nestlé USA

Ortega®, A Division of B&G Foods, Inc.

Reckitt Benckiser Inc.

Sonoma® Dried Tomatoes

Unilever

Walnut Marketing Board

VOLUME MEASUREMENTS (dry)

$1/8$ teaspoon = 0.5 mL
$1/4$ teaspoon = 1 mL
$1/2$ teaspoon = 2 mL
$3/4$ teaspoon = 4 mL
1 teaspoon = 5 mL
1 tablespoon = 15 mL
2 tablespoons = 30 mL
$1/4$ cup = 60 mL
$1/3$ cup = 75 mL
$1/2$ cup = 125 mL
$2/3$ cup = 150 mL
$3/4$ cup = 175 mL
1 cup = 250 mL
2 cups = 1 pint = 500 mL
3 cups = 750 mL
4 cups = 1 quart = 1 L

VOLUME MEASUREMENTS (fluid)

1 fluid ounce (2 tablespoons) = 30 mL
4 fluid ounces ($1/2$ cup) = 125 mL
8 fluid ounces (1 cup) = 250 mL
12 fluid ounces ($1 1/2$ cups) = 375 mL
16 fluid ounces (2 cups) = 500 mL

WEIGHTS (mass)

$1/2$ ounce = 15 g
1 ounce = 30 g
3 ounces = 90 g
4 ounces = 120 g
8 ounces = 225 g
10 ounces = 285 g
12 ounces = 360 g
16 ounces = 1 pound = 450 g

DIMENSIONS

$1/16$ inch = 2 mm
$1/8$ inch = 3 mm
$1/4$ inch = 6 mm
$1/2$ inch = 1.5 cm
$3/4$ inch = 2 cm
1 inch = 2.5 cm

OVEN TEMPERATURES

250°F = 120°C
275°F = 140°C
300°F = 150°C
325°F = 160°C
350°F = 180°C
375°F = 190°C
400°F = 200°C
425°F = 220°C
450°F = 230°C

BAKING PAN SIZES

Utensil	Size in Inches/Quarts	Metric Volume	Size in Centimeters
Baking or Cake Pan (square or rectangular)	$8 \times 8 \times 2$	2 L	$20 \times 20 \times 5$
	$9 \times 9 \times 2$	2.5 L	$23 \times 23 \times 5$
	$12 \times 8 \times 2$	3 L	$30 \times 20 \times 5$
	$13 \times 9 \times 2$	3.5 L	$33 \times 23 \times 5$
Loaf Pan	$8 \times 4 \times 3$	1.5 L	$20 \times 10 \times 7$
	$9 \times 5 \times 3$	2 L	$23 \times 13 \times 7$
Round Layer Cake Pan	$8 \times 1 1/2$	1.2 L	20×4
	$9 \times 1 1/2$	1.5 L	23×4
Pie Plate	$8 \times 1 1/4$	750 mL	20×3
	$9 \times 1 1/4$	1 L	23×3
Baking Dish or Casserole	1 quart	1 L	—
	$1 1/2$ quart	1.5 L	—
	2 quart	2 L	—